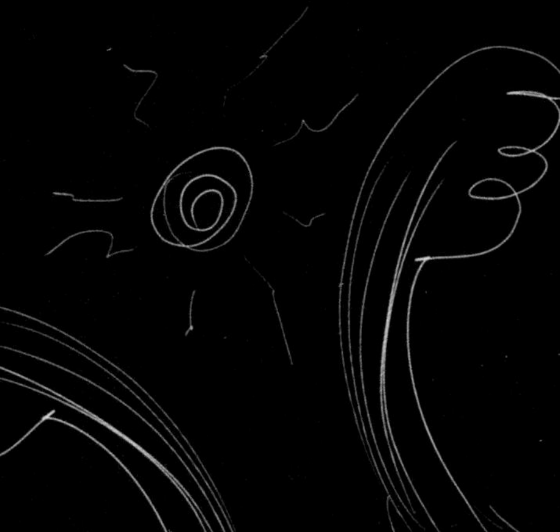

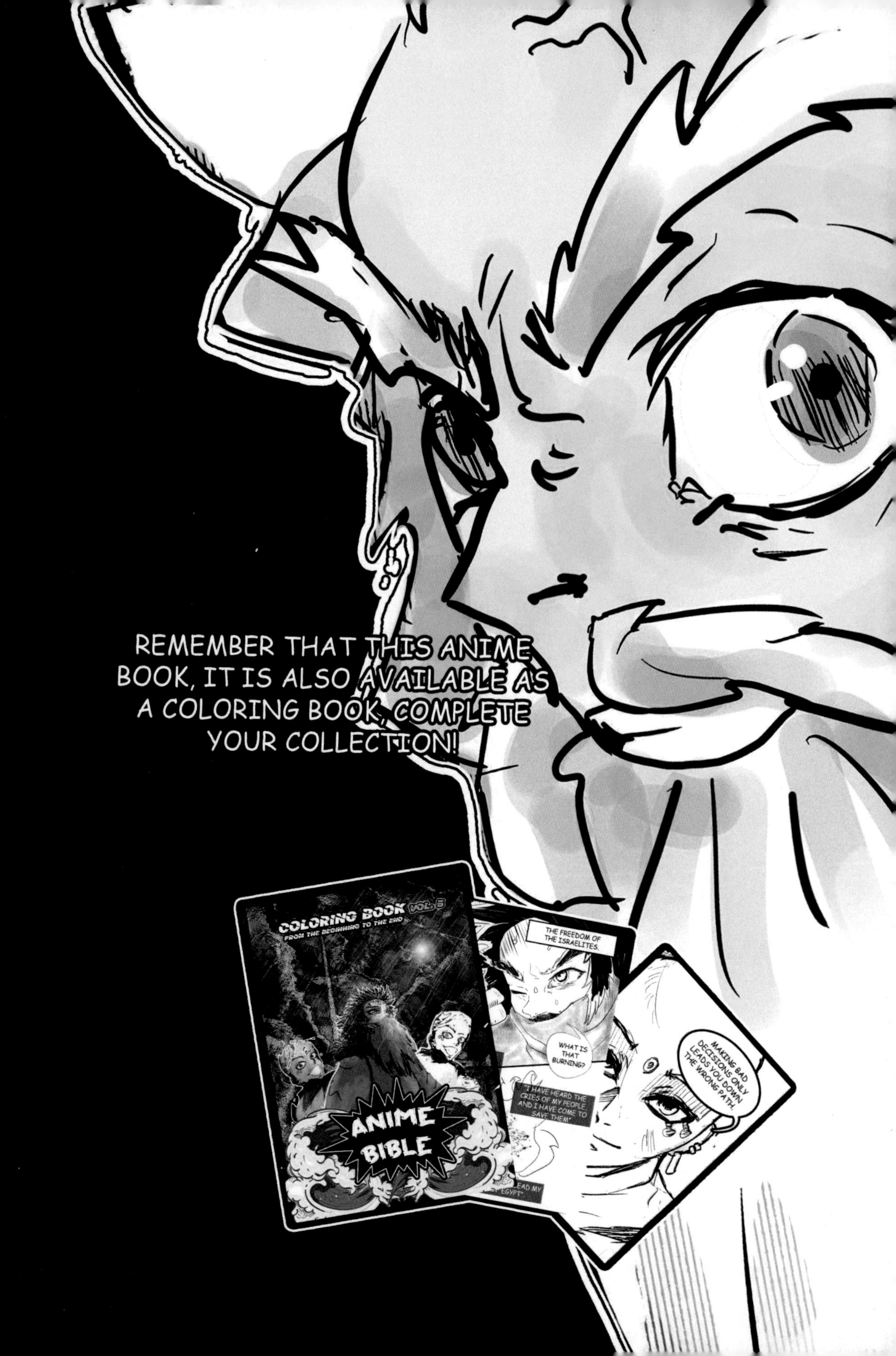

REMEMBER THAT THIS ANIME BOOK, IT IS ALSO AVAILABLE AS A COLORING BOOK, COMPLETE YOUR COLLECTION!
COLORING BOOK vol. 5
FROM THE BEGINNING TO THE END
ANIME BIBLE
THE FREEDOM OF THE ISRAELITES.
WHAT IS THAT BURNING?
"I HAVE HEARD THE CRIES OF MY PEOPLE, AND I HAVE COME TO SAVE THEM"
MAKING BAD DECISIONS ONLY LEADS YOU DOWN THE WRONG PATH.

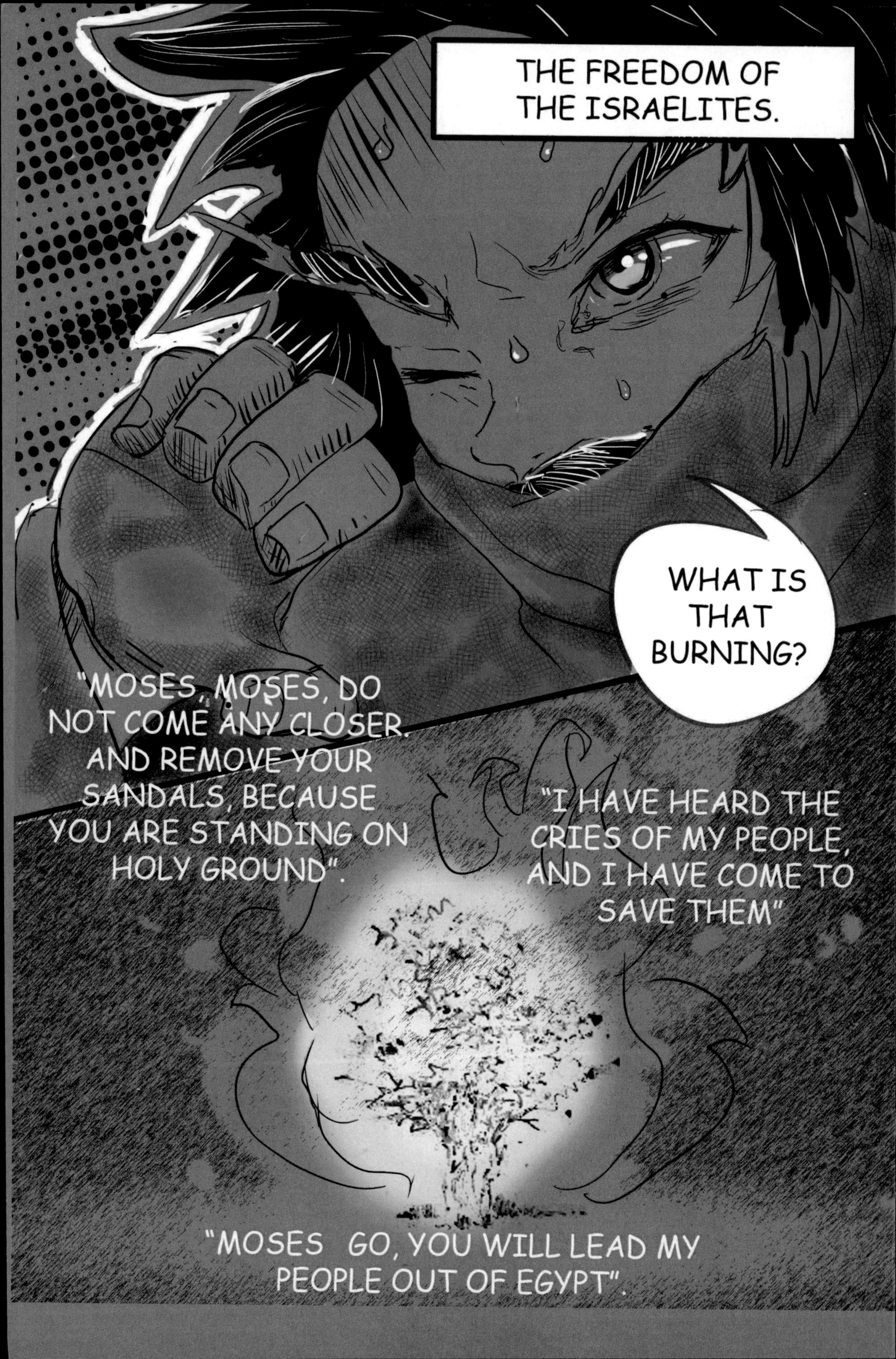
THE FREEDOM OF THE ISRAELITES.
WHAT IS THAT BURNING?
"MOSES, MOSES, DO NOT COME ANY CLOSER. AND REMOVE YOUR SANDALS, BECAUSE YOU ARE STANDING ON HOLY GROUND".
"I HAVE HEARD THE CRIES OF MY PEOPLE, AND I HAVE COME TO SAVE THEM"
"MOSES GO, YOU WILL LEAD MY PEOPLE OUT OF EGYPT".

THE PHARAOH WOULD HAVE NEVER EXPECTED WHAT WAS ABOUT TO HAPPEN
MOSES ARRIVED WITH THE EMPOWERMENT GIVEN BY GOD TO GET HIS PEOPLE OUT OF MISERY.

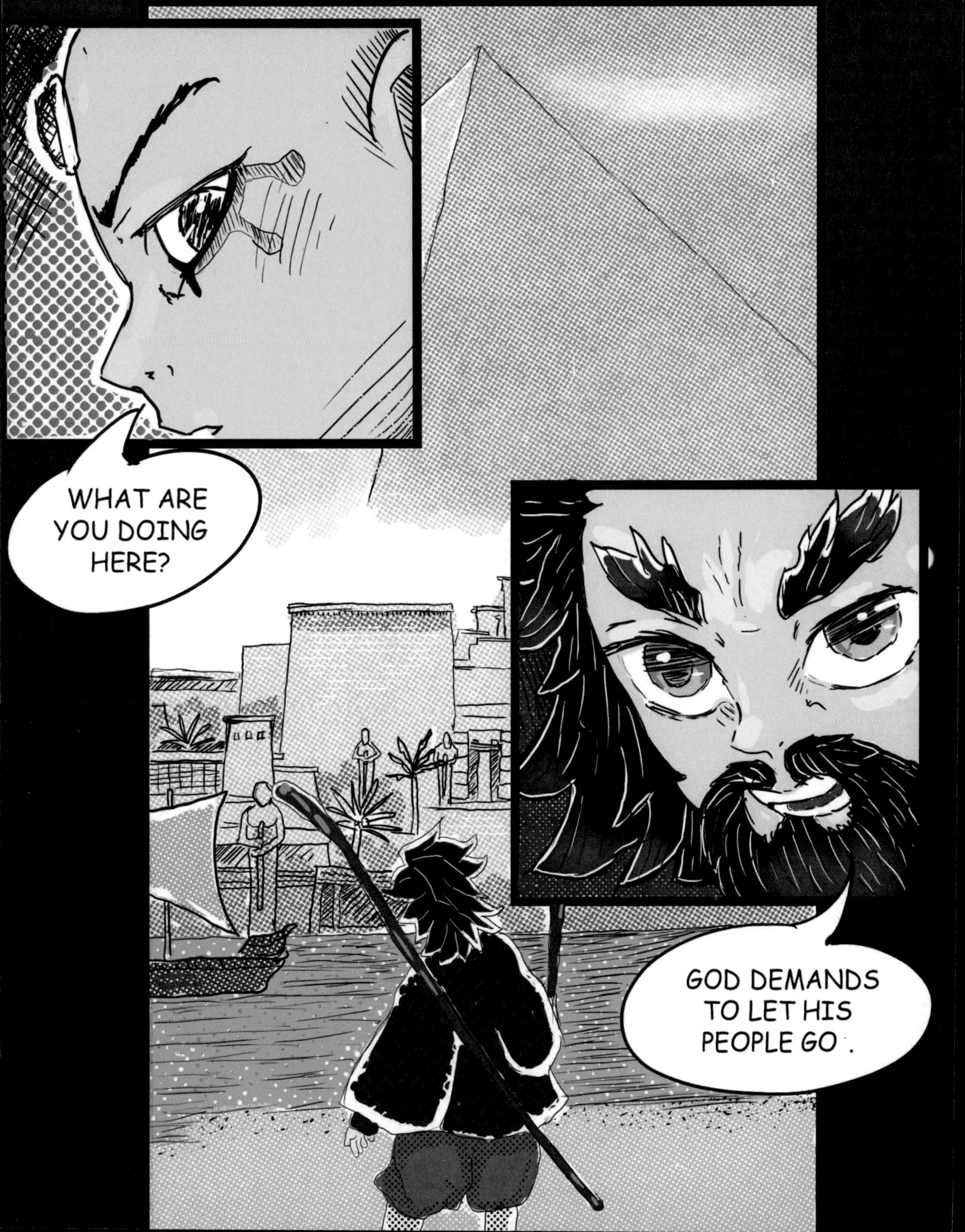
WHAT ARE YOU DOING HERE?
GOD DEMANDS TO LET HIS PEOPLE GO .

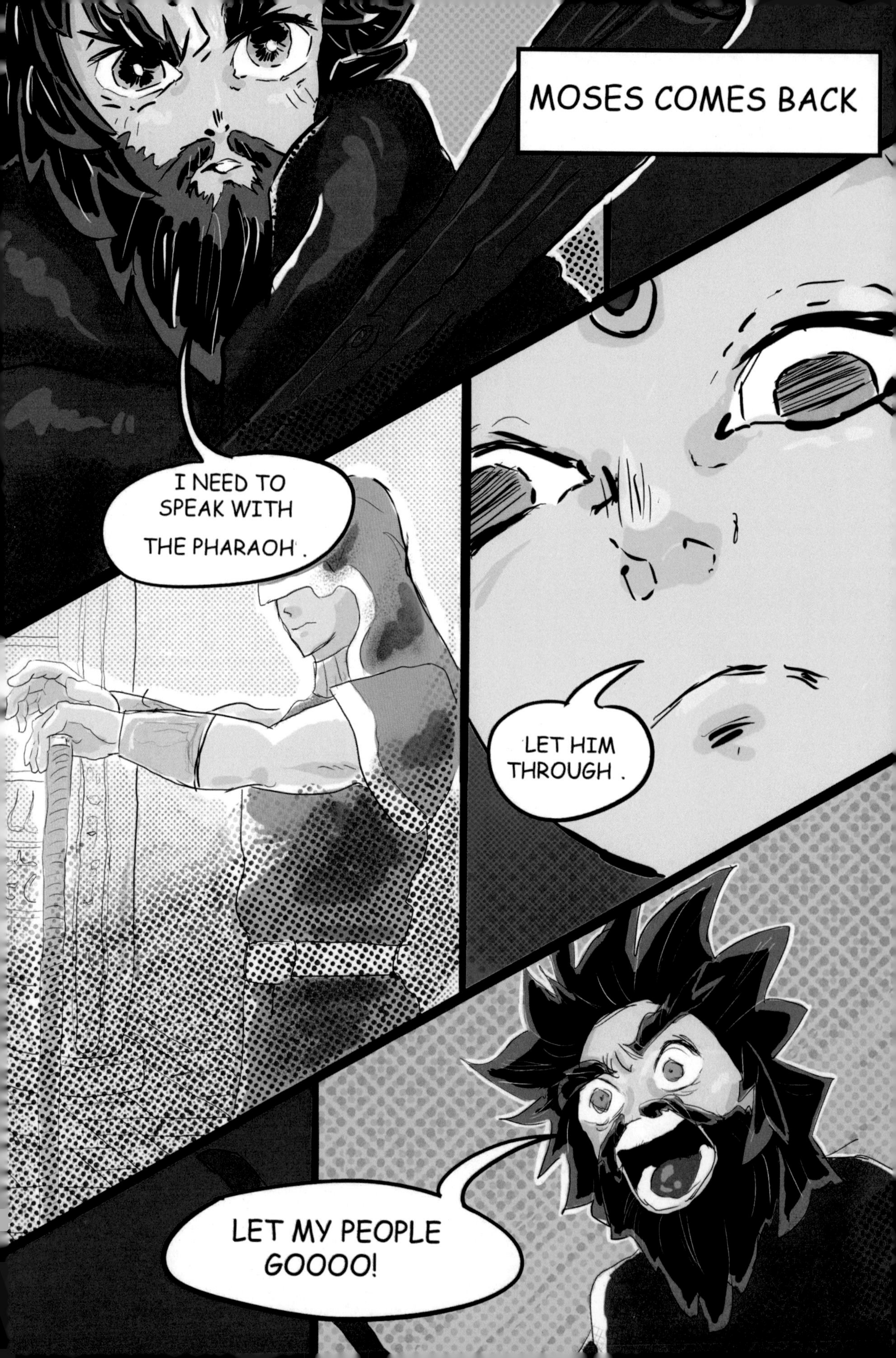
MOSES COMES BACK
I NEED TO SPEAK WITH THE PHARAOH.
LET HIM THROUGH.
LET MY PEOPLE GOOOO!

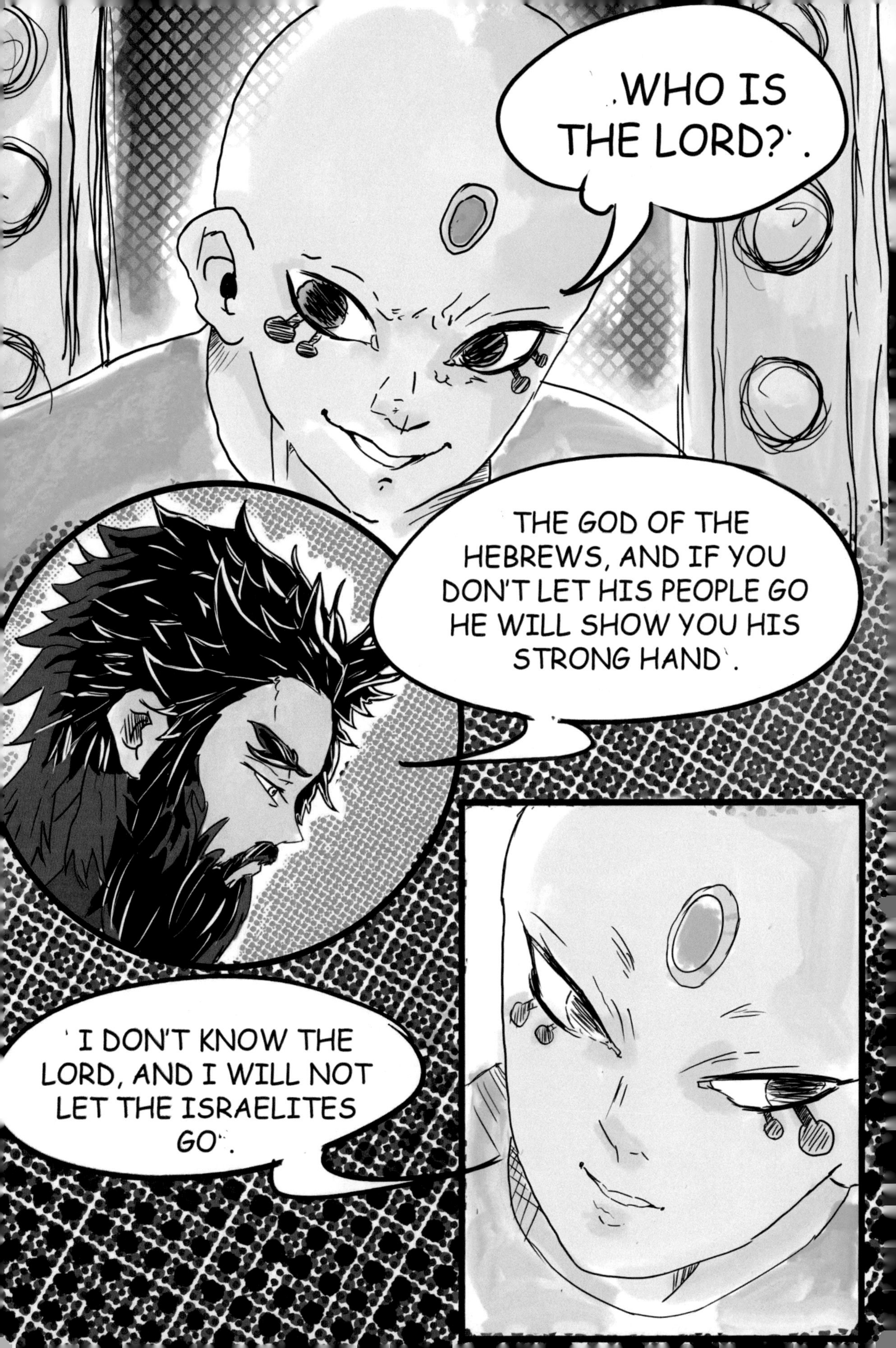
.WHO IS THE LORD?`.
THE GOD OF THE HEBREWS, AND IF YOU DON'T LET HIS PEOPLE GO HE WILL SHOW YOU HIS STRONG HAND`.
' I DON'T KNOW THE LORD, AND I WILL NOT LET THE ISRAELITES GO`.

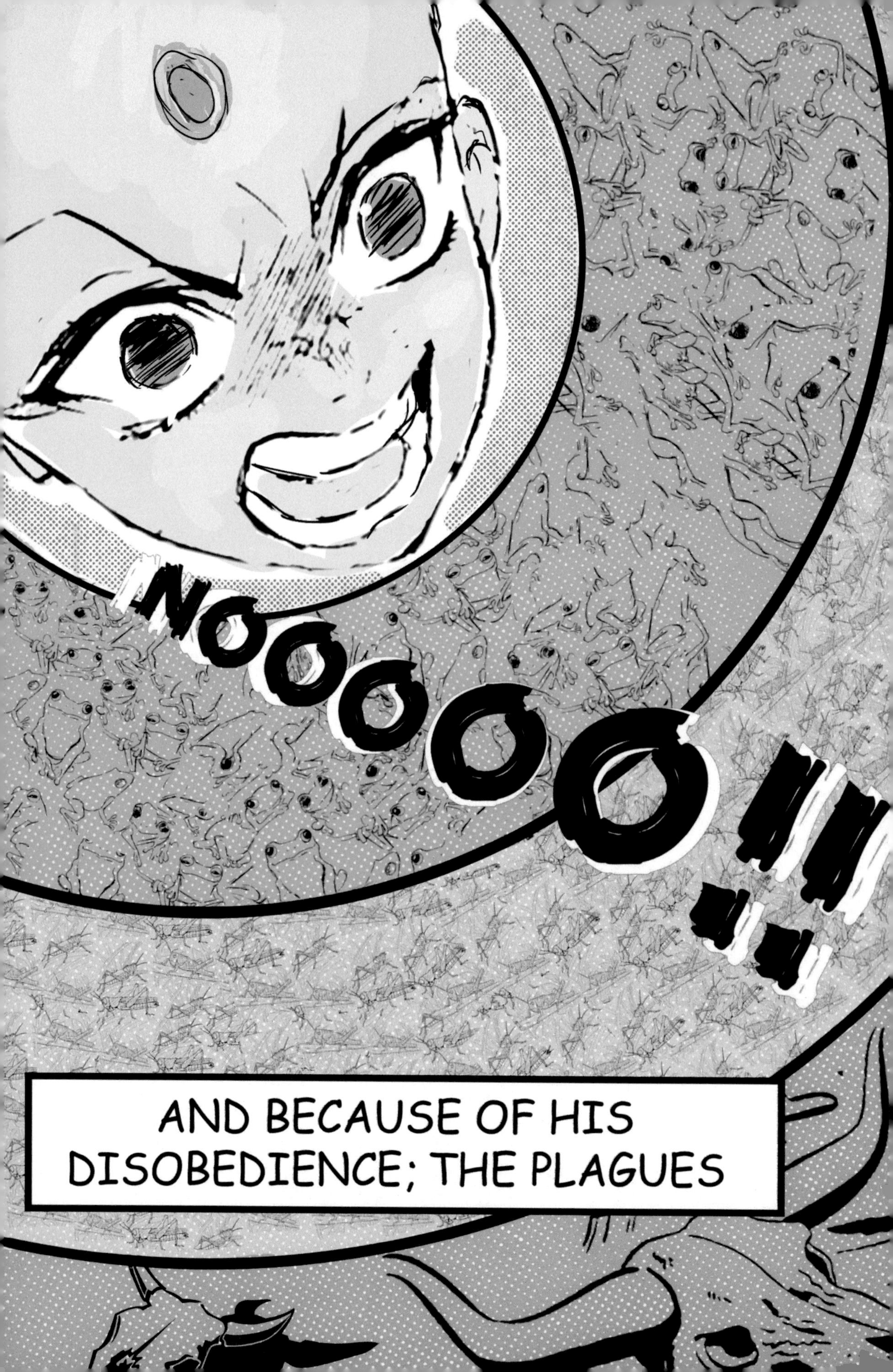
NOOOOO!!!
AND BECAUSE OF HIS DISOBEDIENCE; THE PLAGUES

THE NILE RIVER TURNED INTO BLOOD.

AHHHHHHHHHHHHHH!!!

AND GOD SENT A TREMENDOUS HAILSTORM.

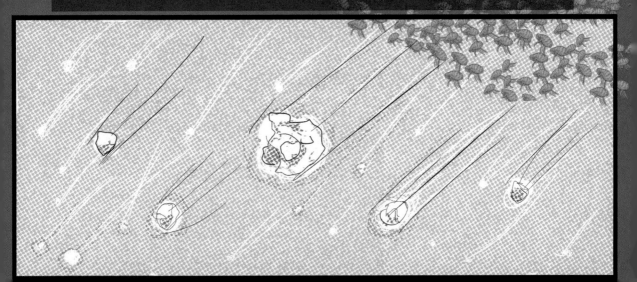

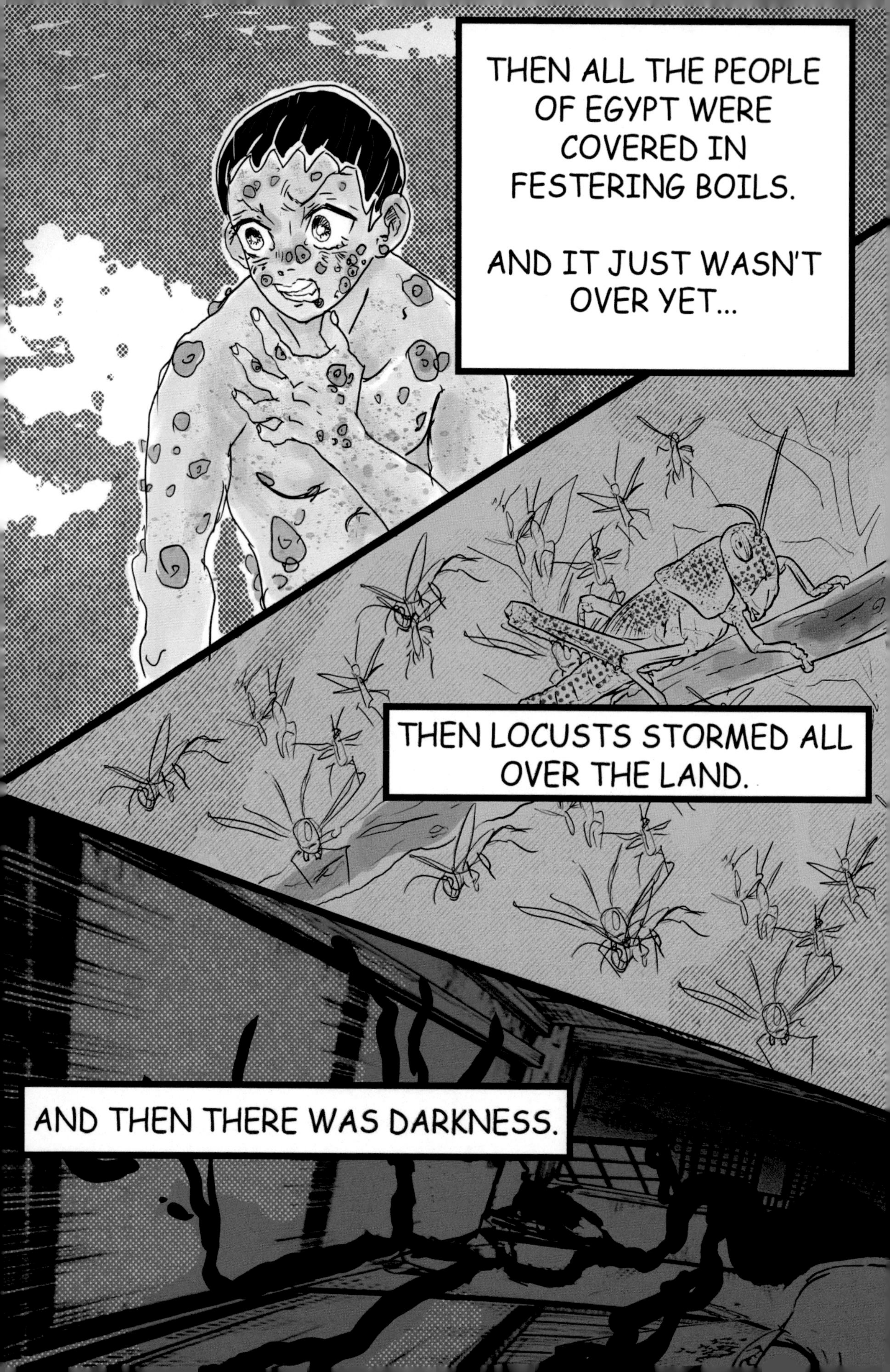
THEN ALL THE PEOPLE OF EGYPT WERE COVERED IN FESTERING BOILS.
AND IT JUST WASN'T OVER YET...
THEN LOCUSTS STORMED ALL OVER THE LAND.
AND THEN THERE WAS DARKNESS.

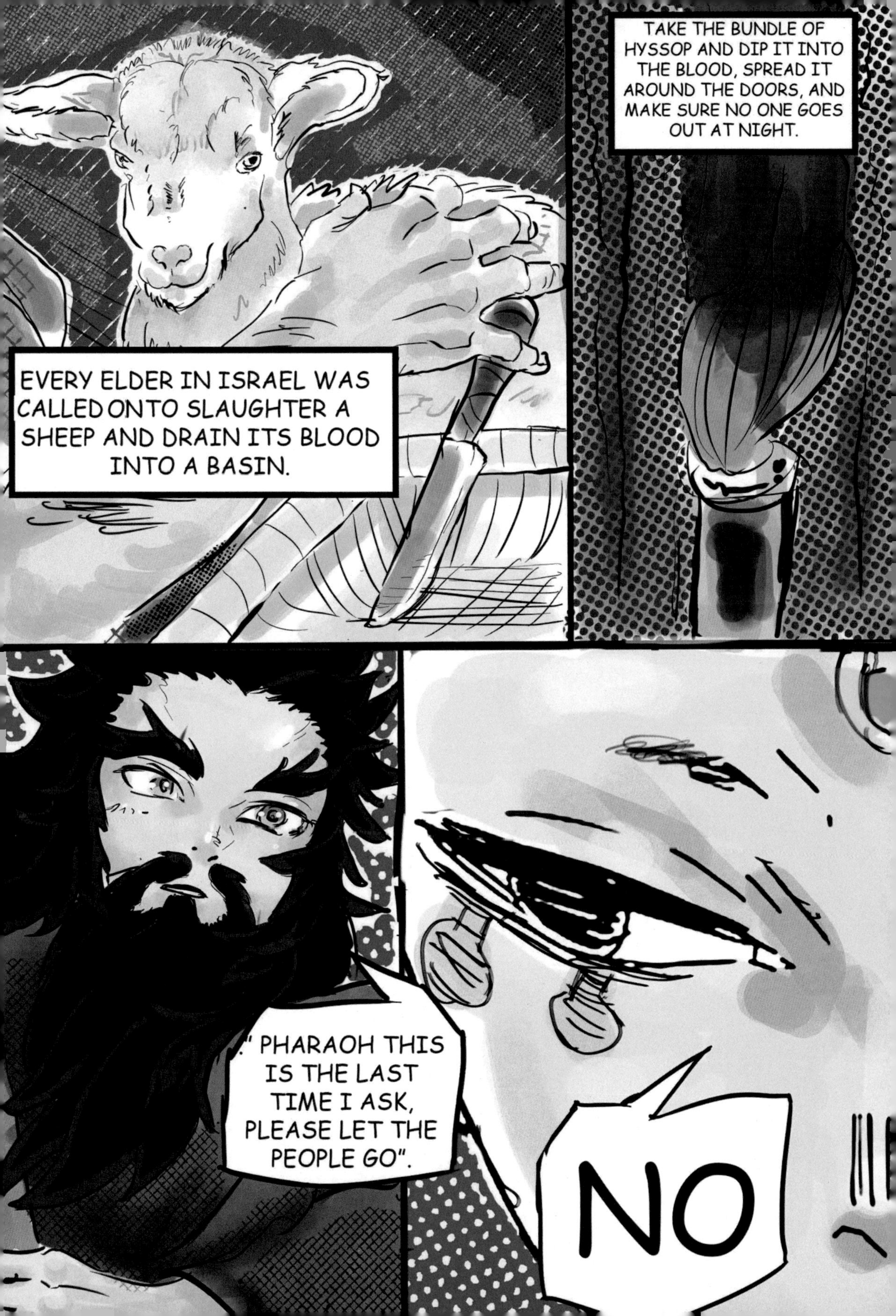
EVERY ELDER IN ISRAEL WAS CALLED ONTO SLAUGHTER A SHEEP AND DRAIN ITS BLOOD INTO A BASIN.
TAKE THE BUNDLE OF HYSSOP AND DIP IT INTO THE BLOOD, SPREAD IT AROUND THE DOORS, AND MAKE SURE NO ONE GOES OUT AT NIGHT.
" PHARAOH THIS IS THE LAST TIME I ASK, PLEASE LET THE PEOPLE GO".
NO

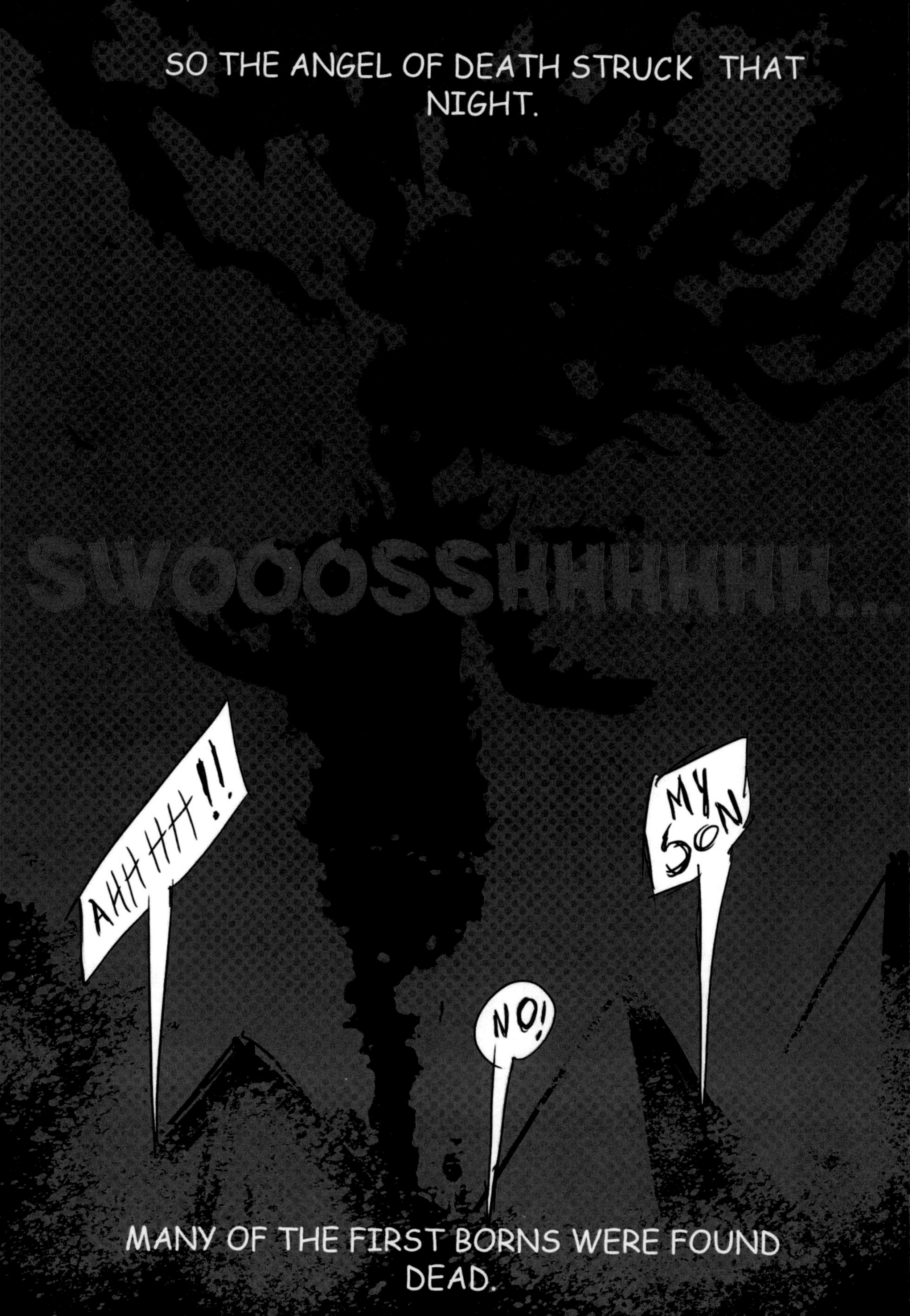
SO THE ANGEL OF DEATH STRUCK THAT NIGHT.
SVOOOSSHHHHHH...
AHHHH!!
MY SON
NO!
MANY OF THE FIRST BORNS WERE FOUND DEAD.

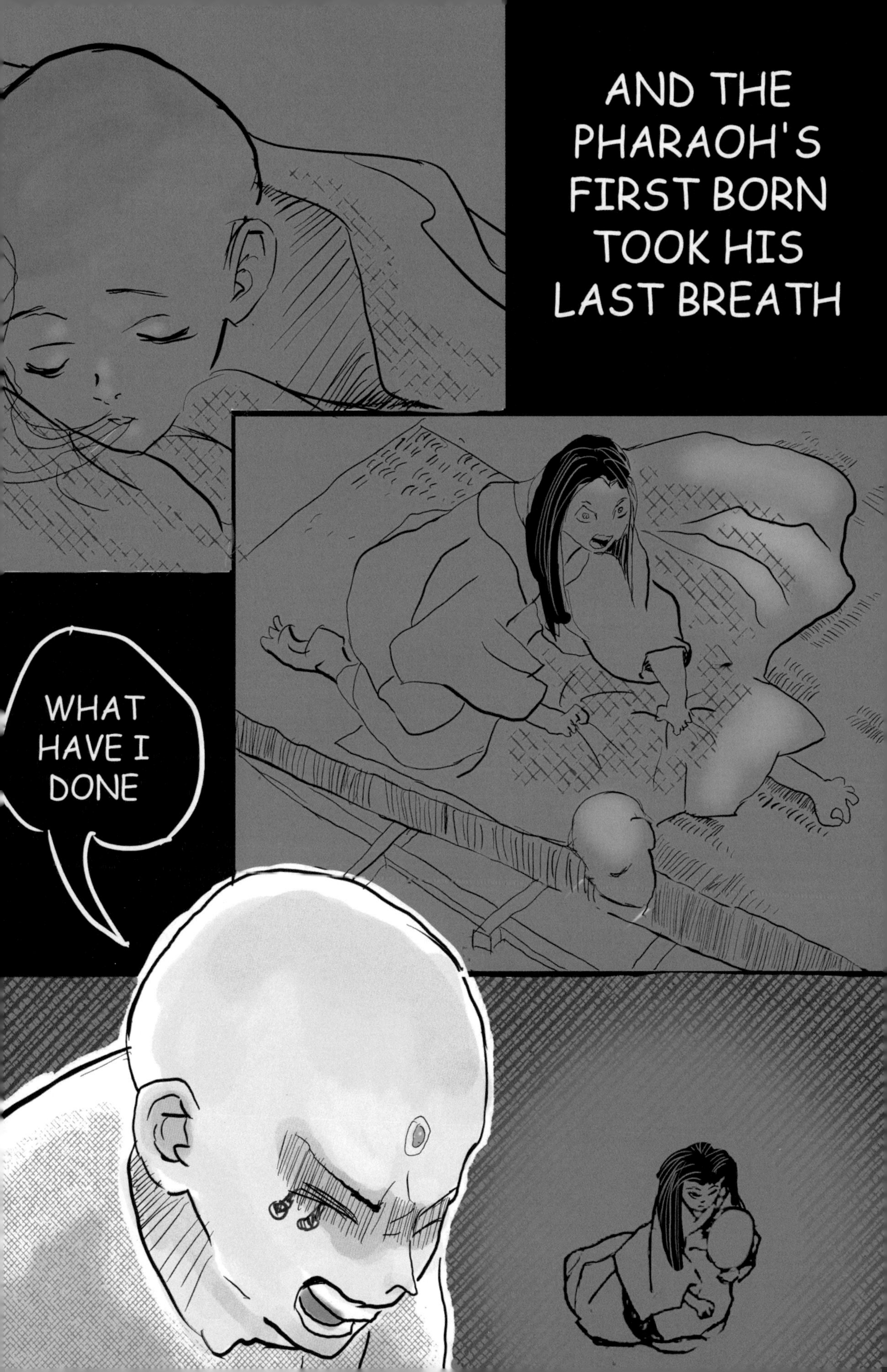
AND THE PHARAOH'S FIRST BORN TOOK HIS LAST BREATH
WHAT HAVE I DONE

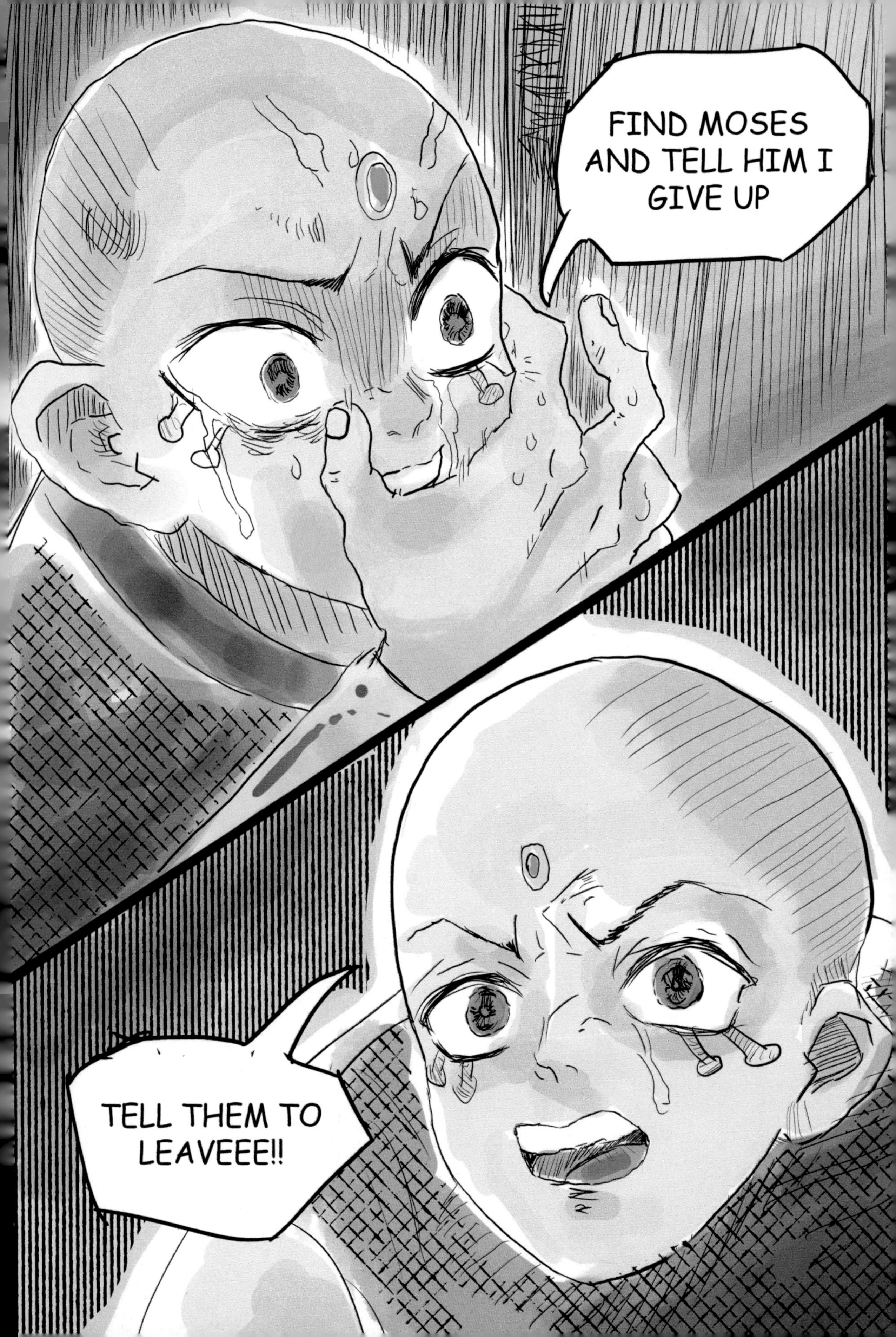
FIND MOSES AND TELL HIM I GIVE UP
TELL THEM TO LEAVEEE!!

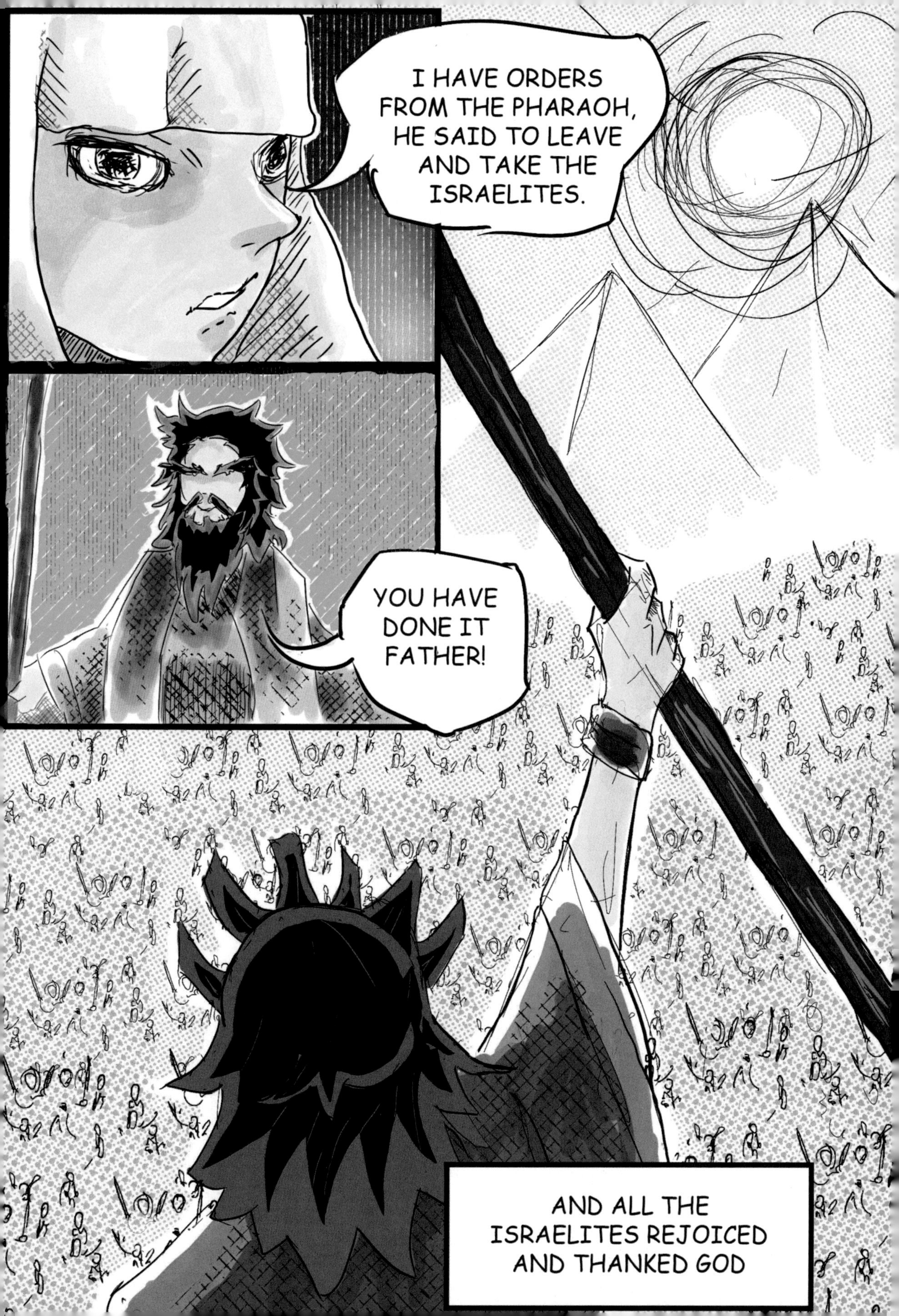
I HAVE ORDERS FROM THE PHARAOH, HE SAID TO LEAVE AND TAKE THE ISRAELITES.
YOU HAVE DONE IT FATHER!
AND ALL THE ISRAELITES REJOICED AND THANKED GOD

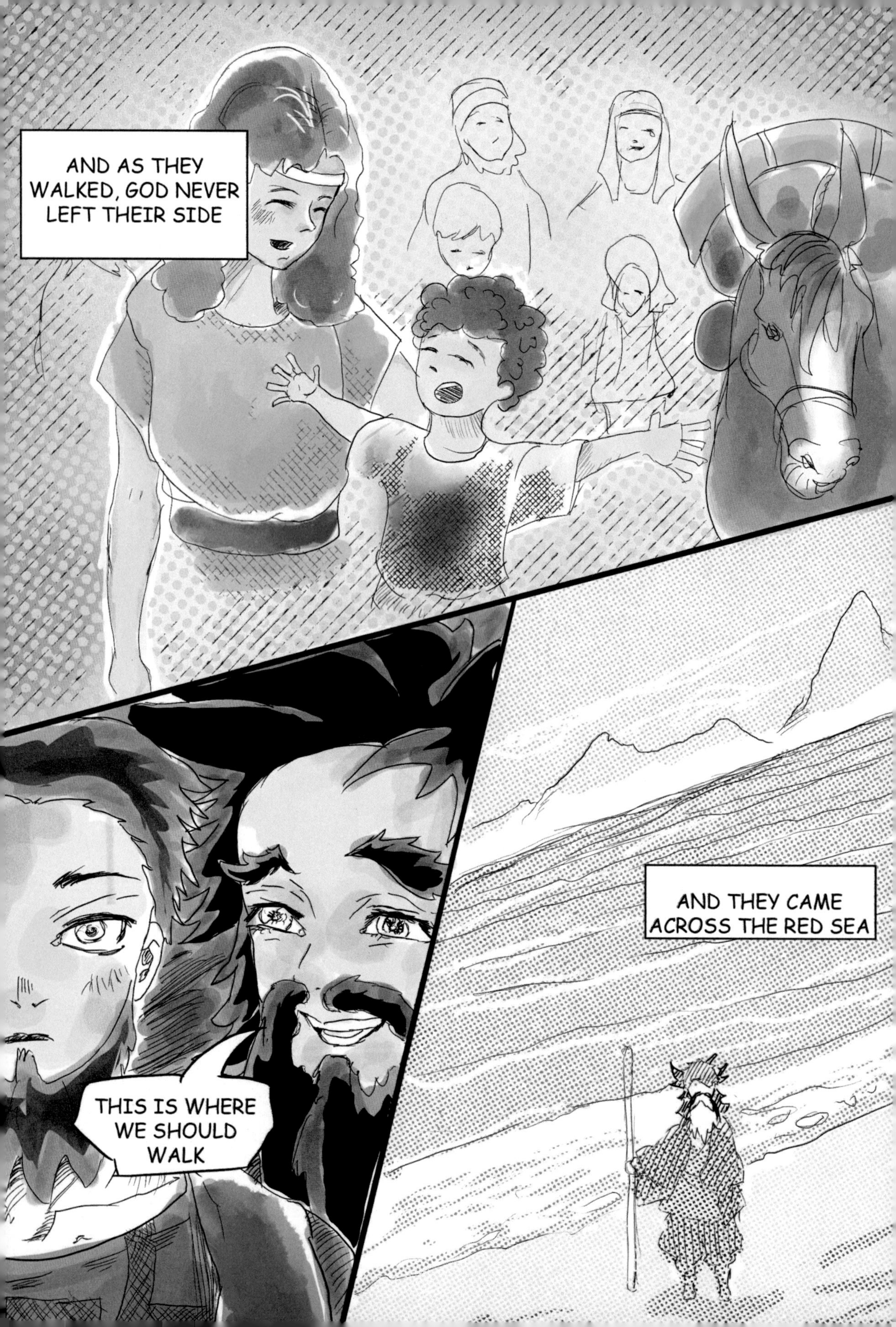
AND AS THEY WALKED, GOD NEVER LEFT THEIR SIDE
AND THEY CAME ACROSS THE RED SEA
THIS IS WHERE WE SHOULD WALK

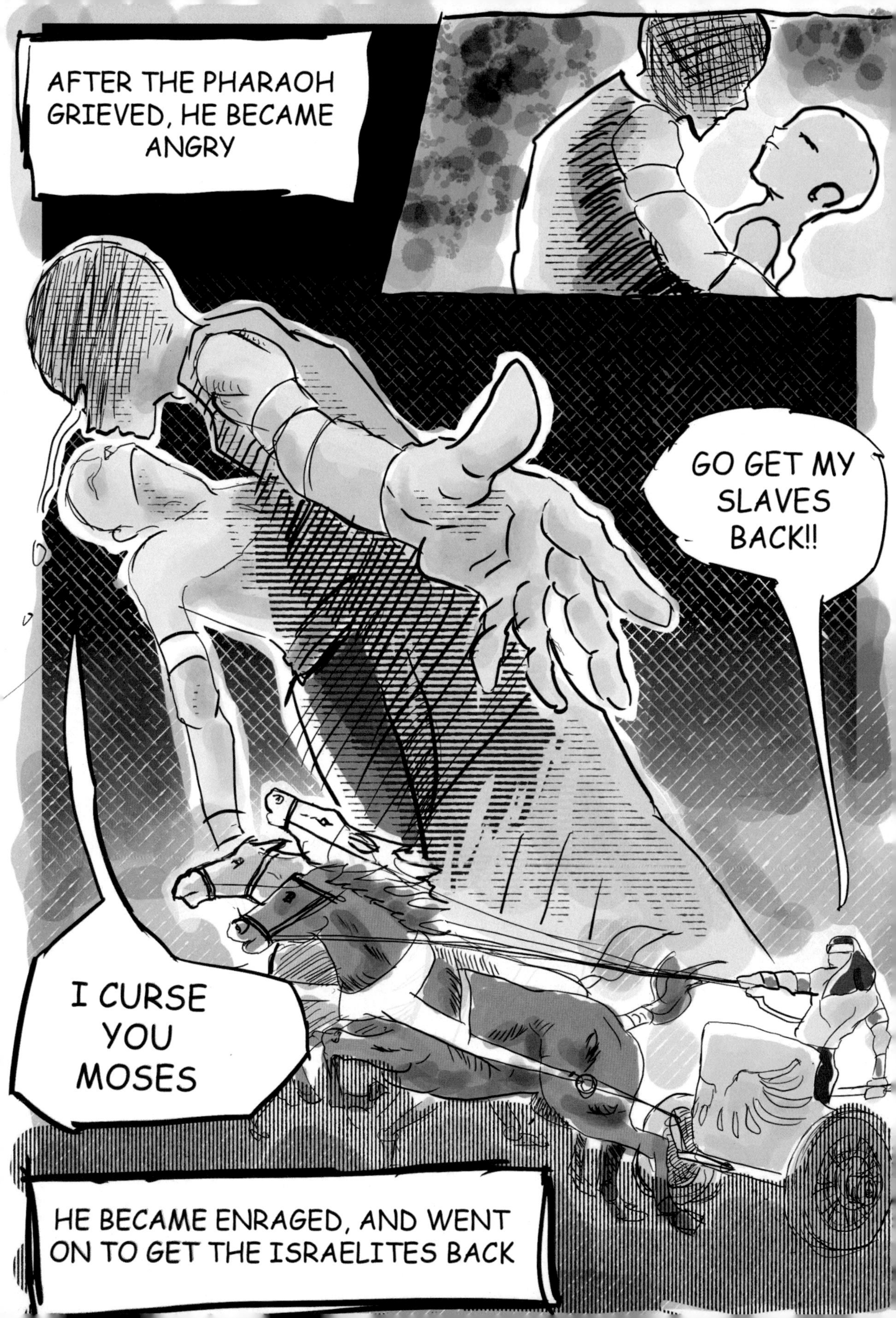
AFTER THE PHARAOH GRIEVED, HE BECAME ANGRY
GO GET MY SLAVES BACK!!
I CURSE YOU MOSES
HE BECAME ENRAGED, AND WENT ON TO GET THE ISRAELITES BACK

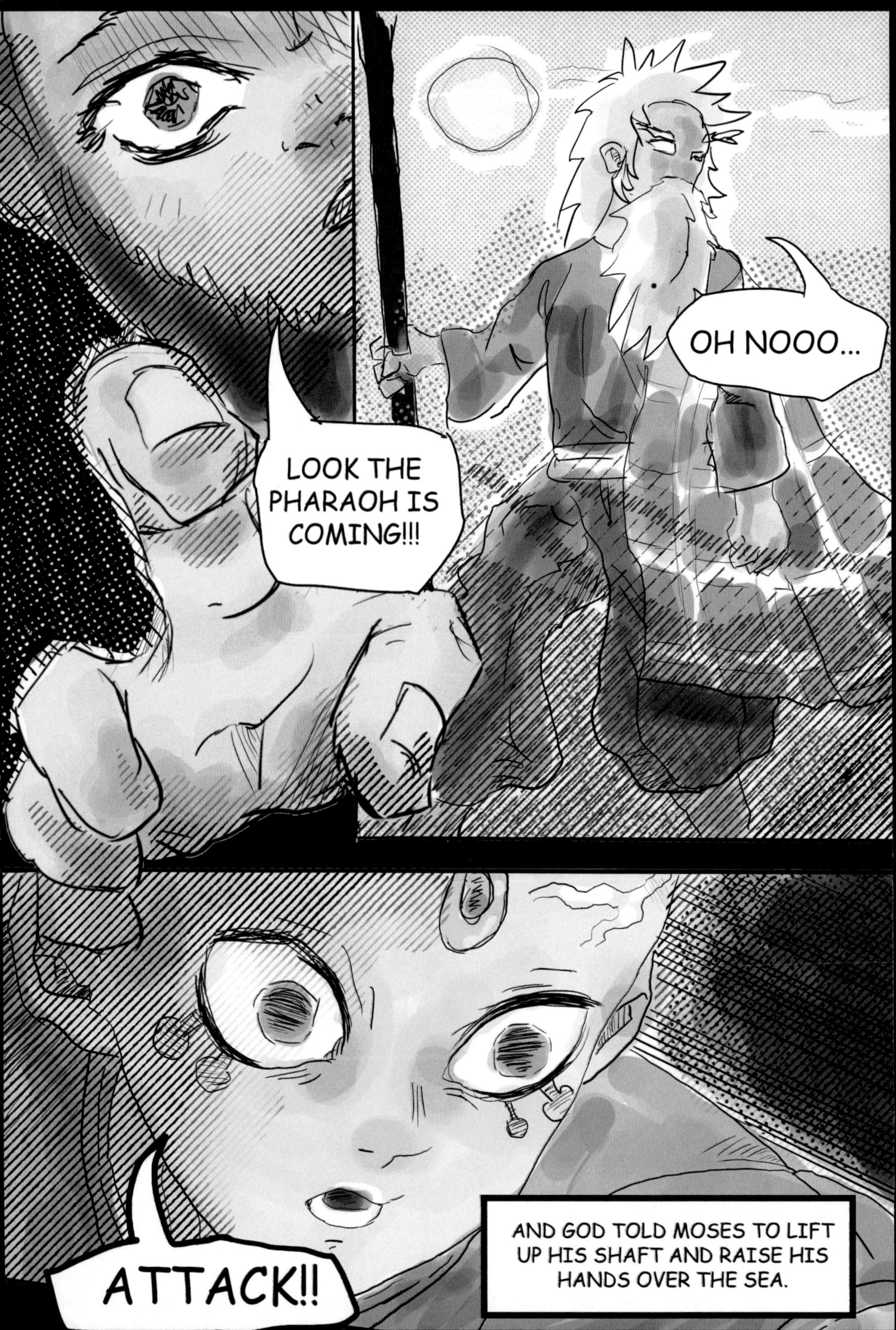
OH NOOO...
LOOK THE PHARAOH IS COMING!!!
ATTACK!!
AND GOD TOLD MOSES TO LIFT UP HIS SHAFT AND RAISE HIS HANDS OVER THE SEA.

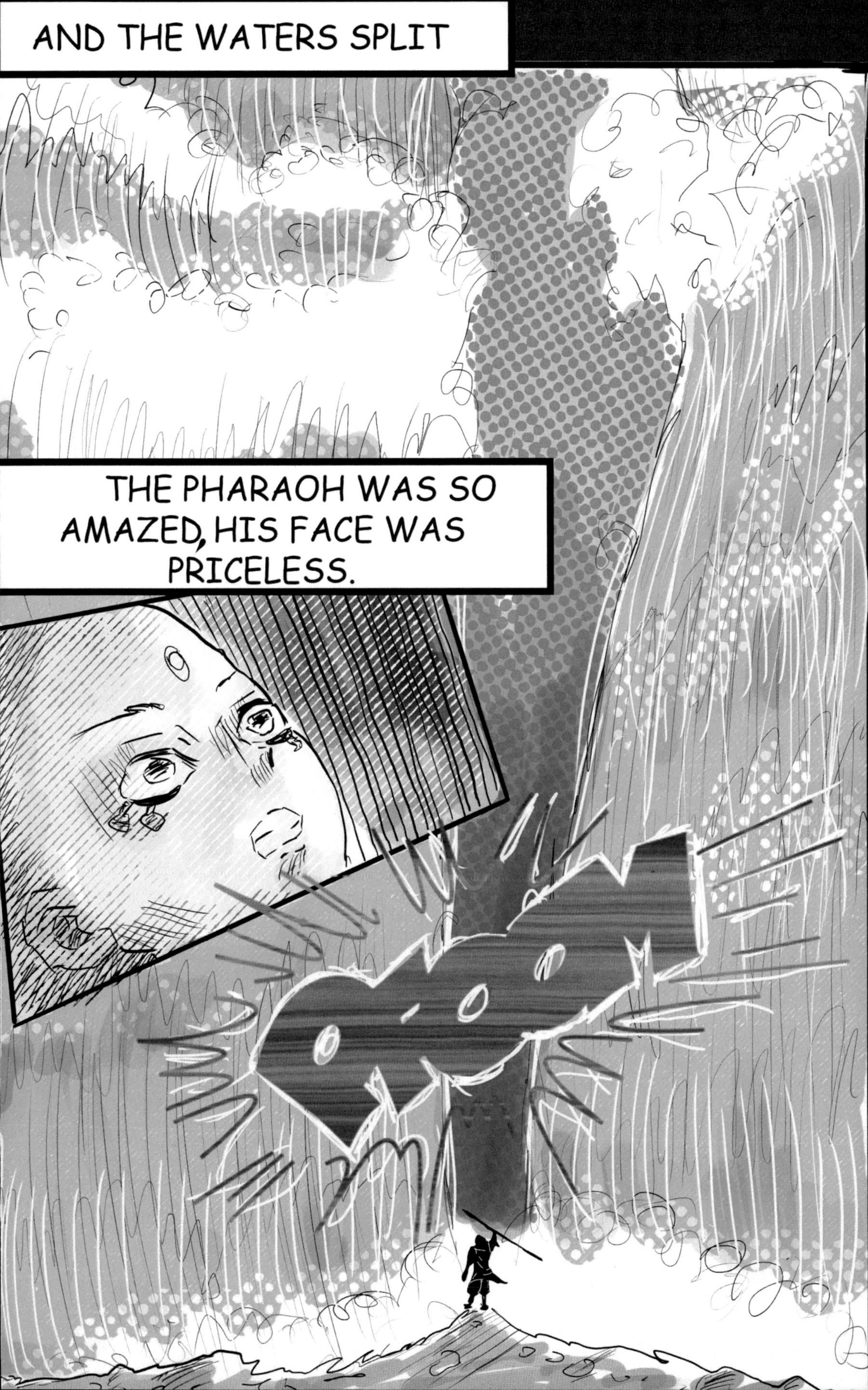
AND THE WATERS SPLIT
THE PHARAOH WAS SO AMAZED, HIS FACE WAS PRICELESS.

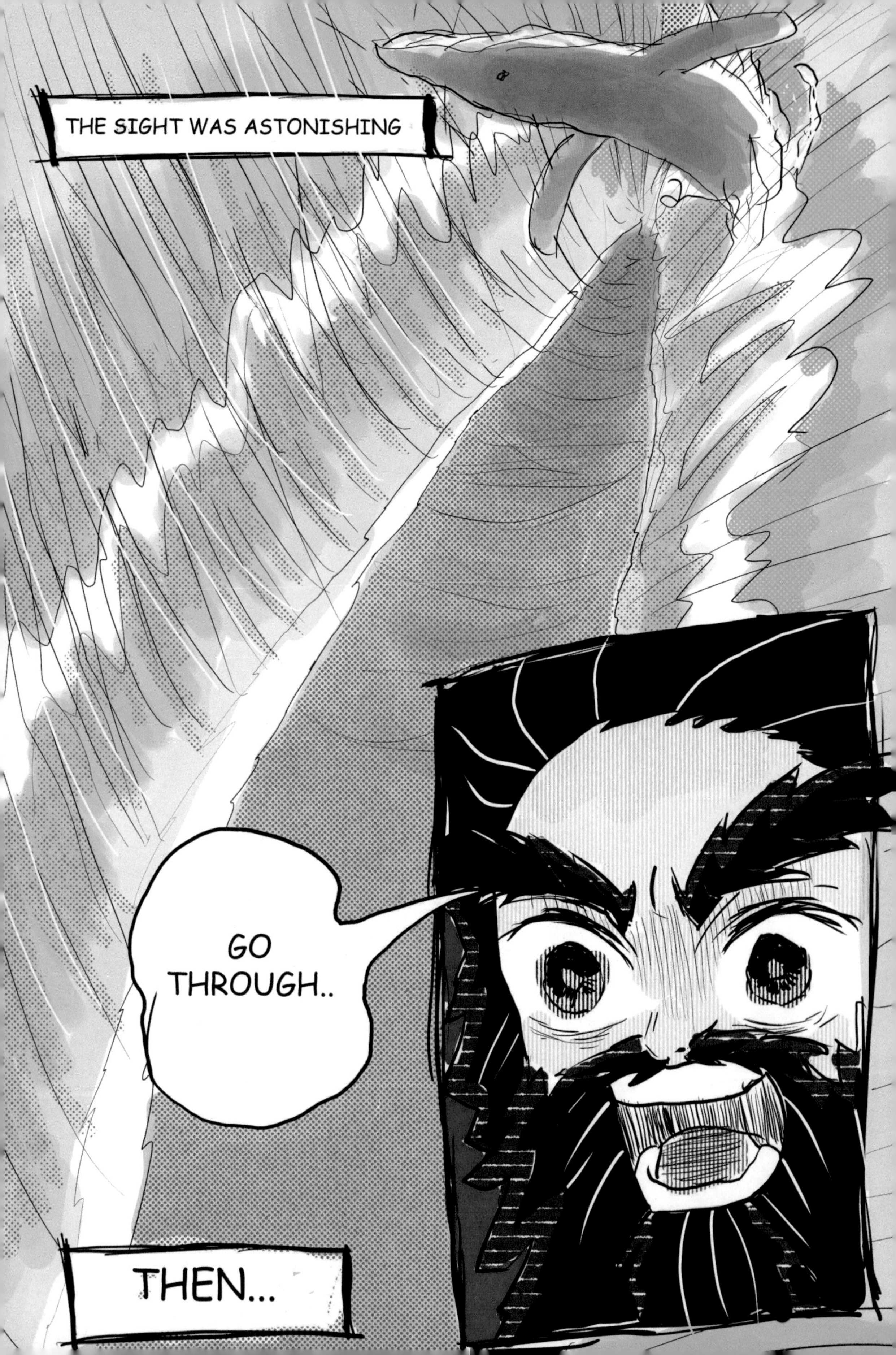
THE SIGHT WAS ASTONISHING
GO THROUGH..
THEN...

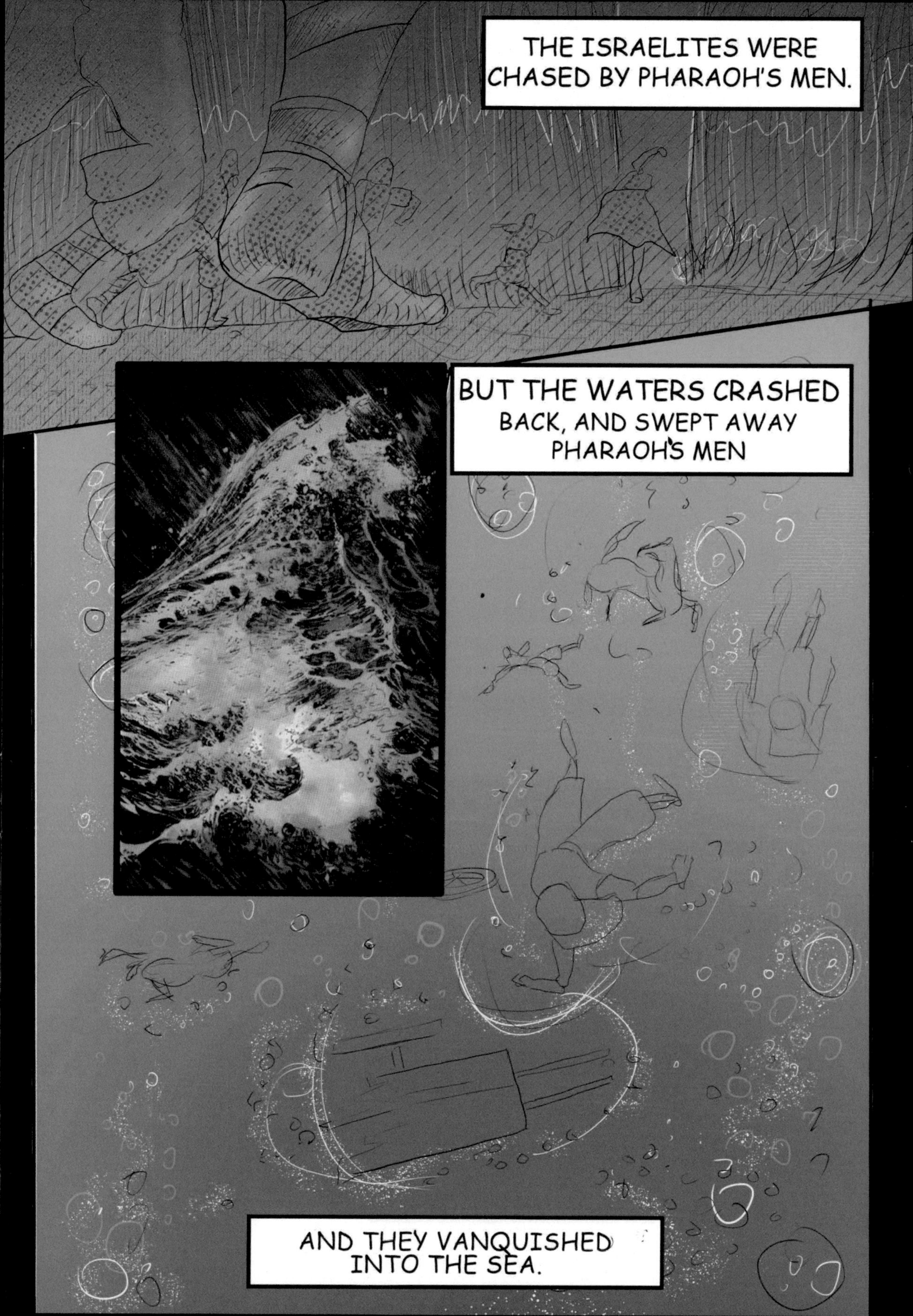
THE ISRAELITES WERE CHASED BY PHARAOH'S MEN.
BUT THE WATERS CRASHED BACK, AND SWEPT AWAY PHARAOH'S MEN
AND THEY VANQUISHED INTO THE SEA.

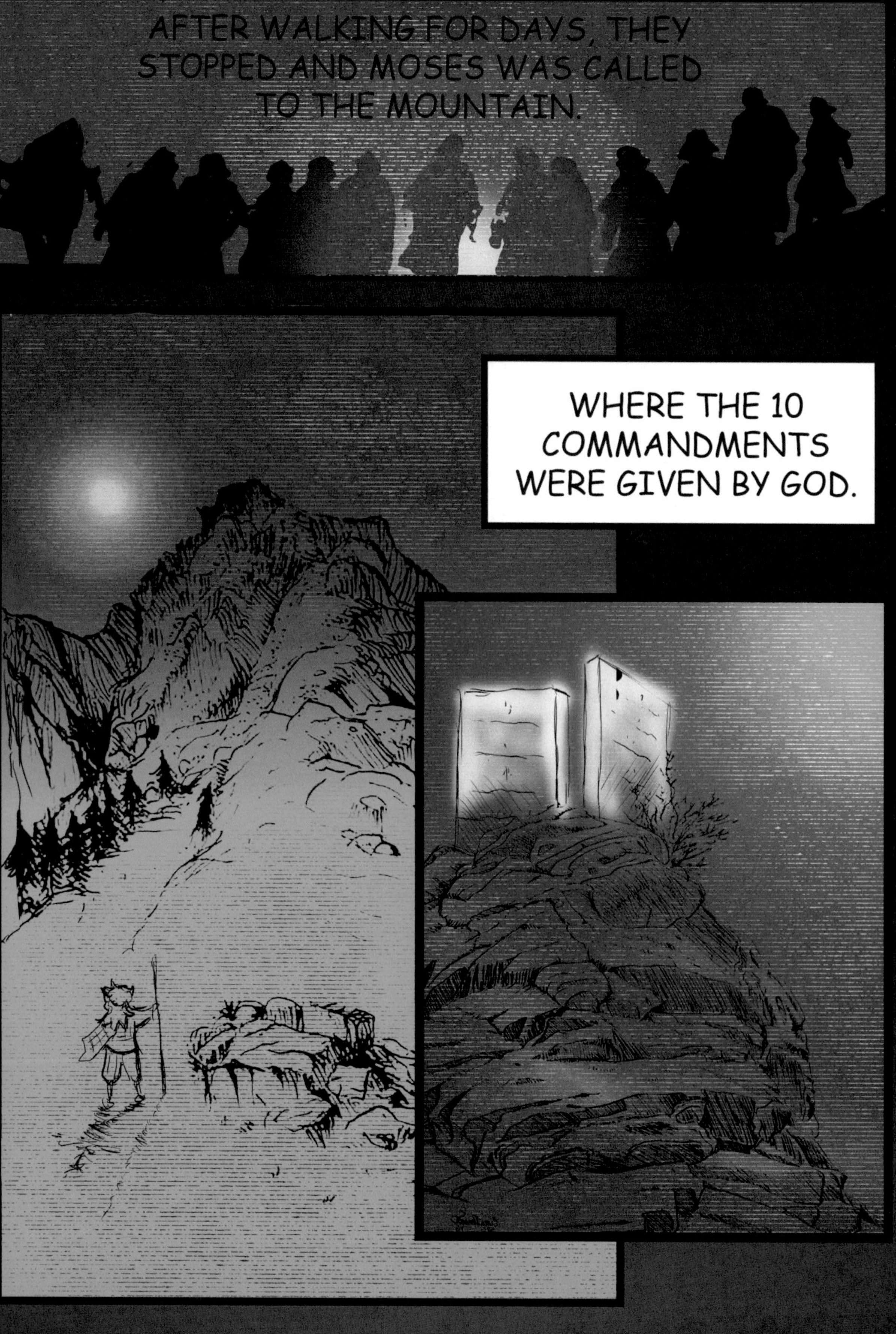
AFTER WALKING FOR DAYS, THEY STOPPED AND MOSES WAS CALLED TO THE MOUNTAIN.
WHERE THE 10 COMMANDMENTS WERE GIVEN BY GOD.

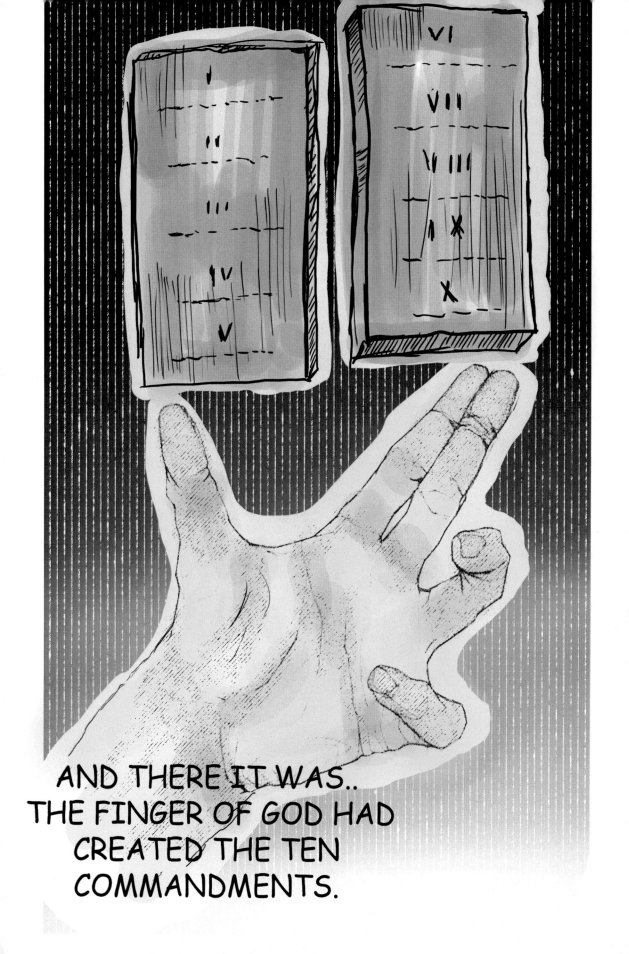

AND THERE IT WAS..
THE FINGER OF GOD HAD
CREATED THE TEN
COMMANDMENTS.

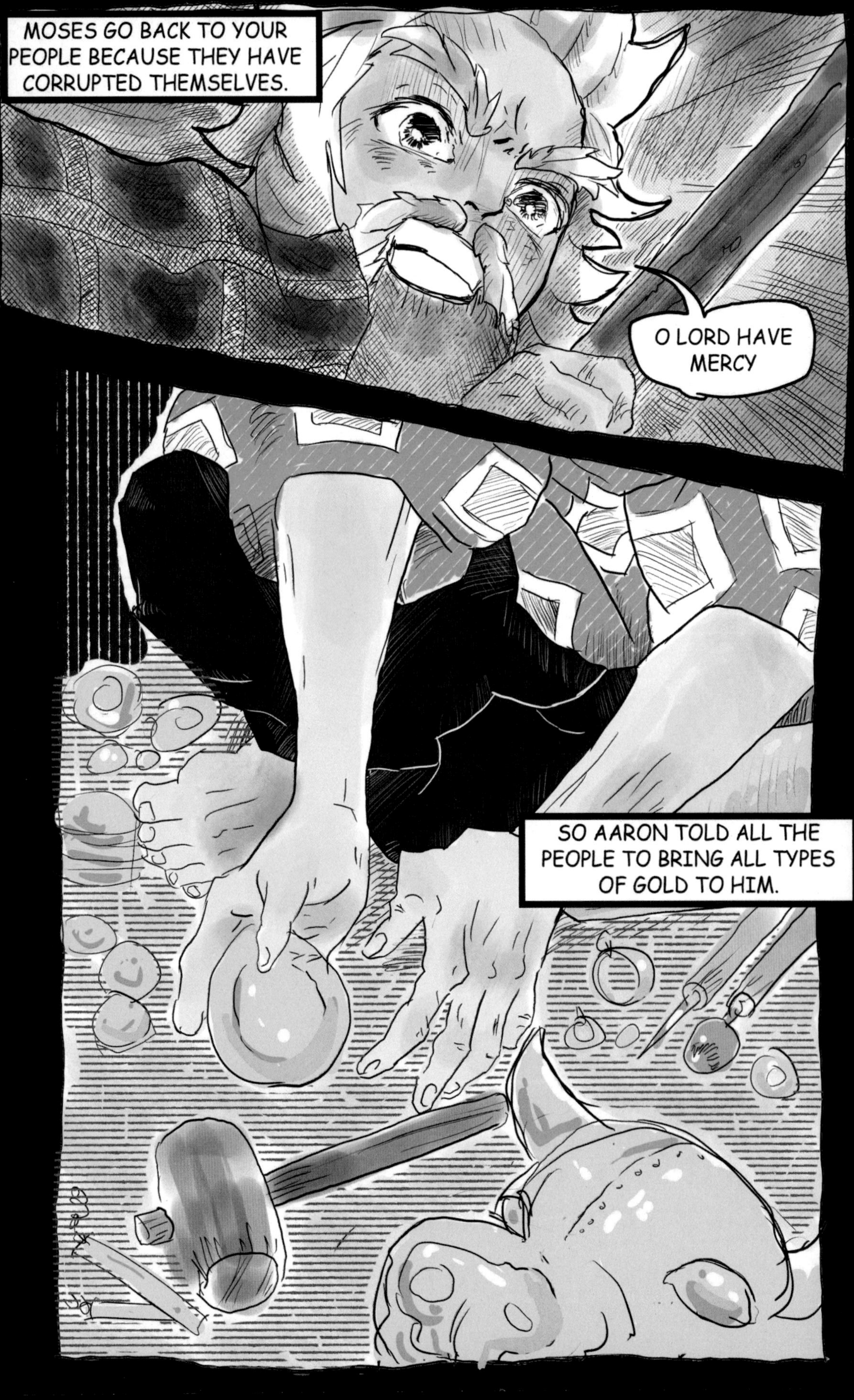
MOSES GO BACK TO YOUR PEOPLE BECAUSE THEY HAVE CORRUPTED THEMSELVES.
O LORD HAVE MERCY
SO AARON TOLD ALL THE PEOPLE TO BRING ALL TYPES OF GOLD TO HIM.

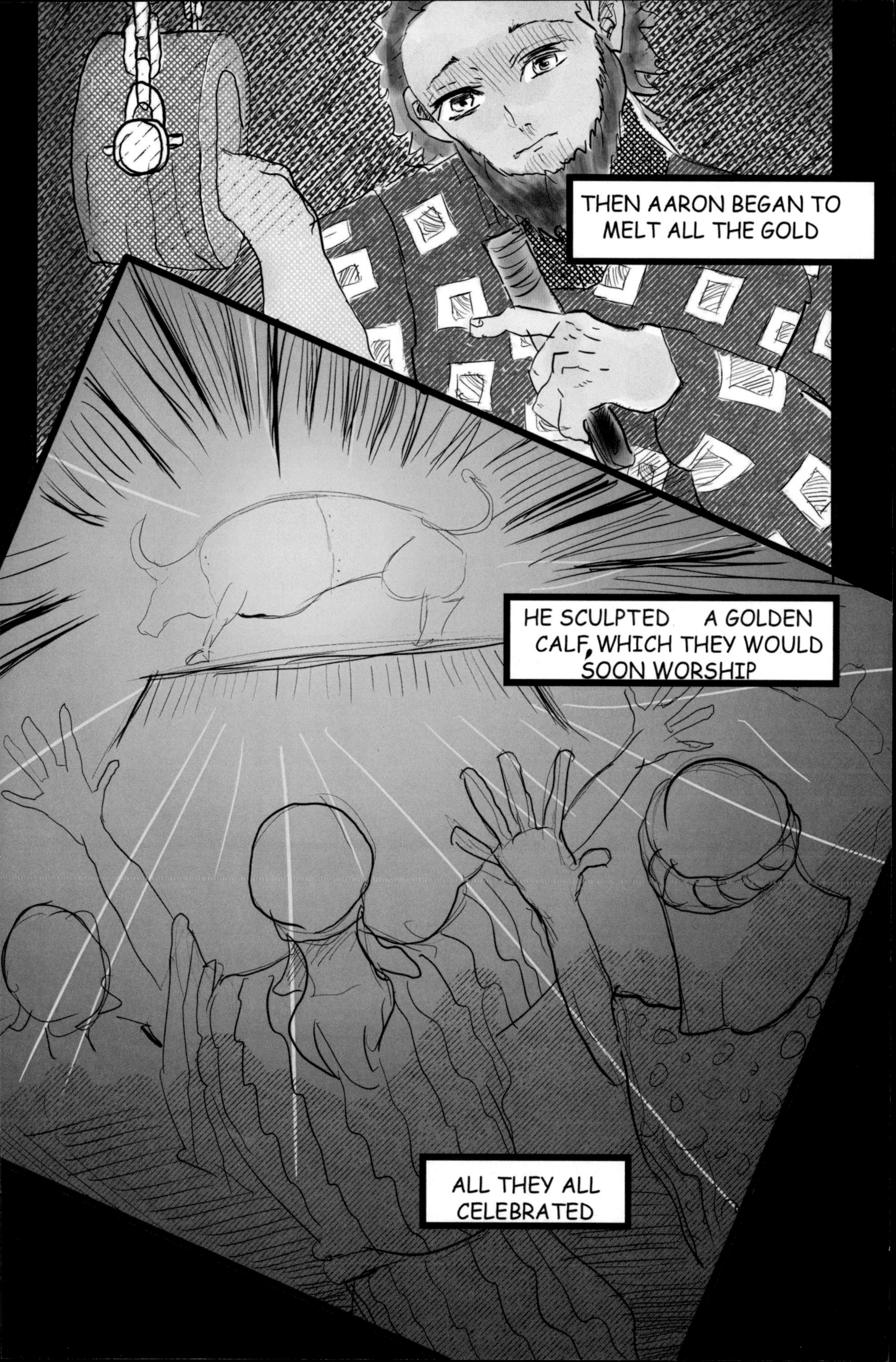
THEN AARON BEGAN TO MELT ALL THE GOLD
HE SCULPTED A GOLDEN CALF, WHICH THEY WOULD SOON WORSHIP
ALL THEY ALL CELEBRATED

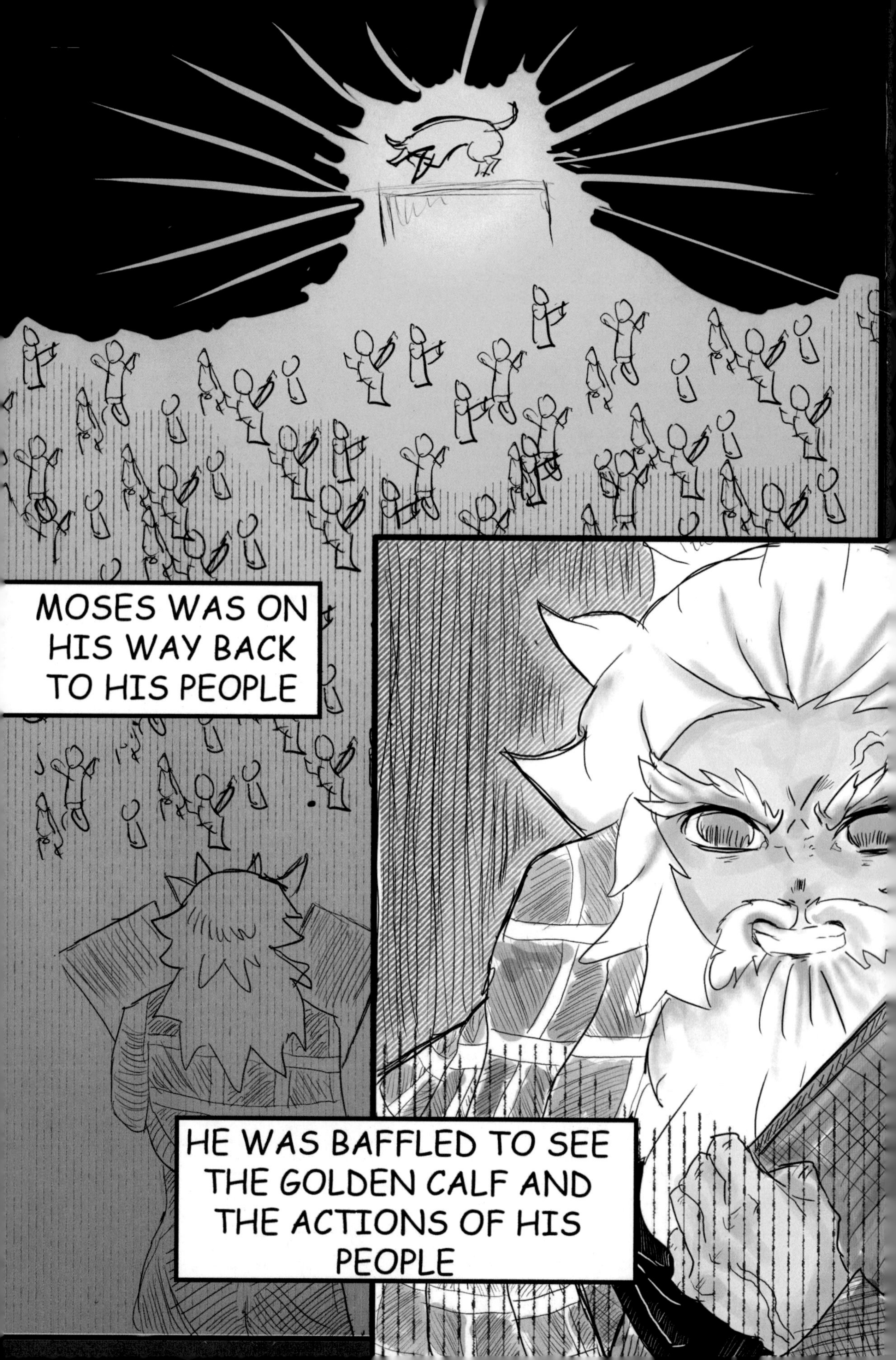
MOSES WAS ON
HIS WAY BACK
TO HIS PEOPLE
HE WAS BAFFLED TO SEE
THE GOLDEN CALF AND
THE ACTIONS OF HIS
PEOPLE

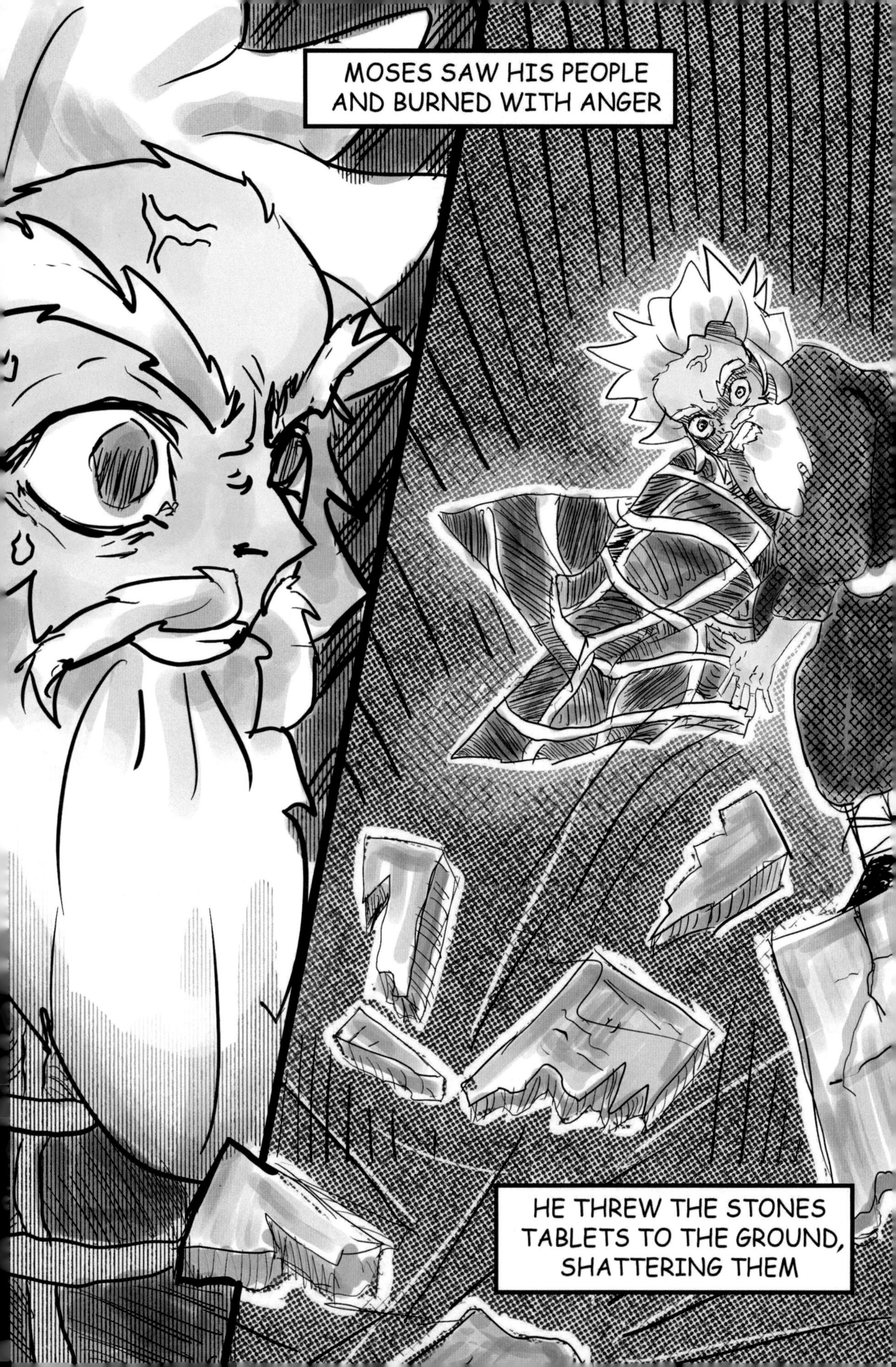
MOSES SAW HIS PEOPLE AND BURNED WITH ANGER
HE THREW THE STONES TABLETS TO THE GROUND, SHATTERING THEM

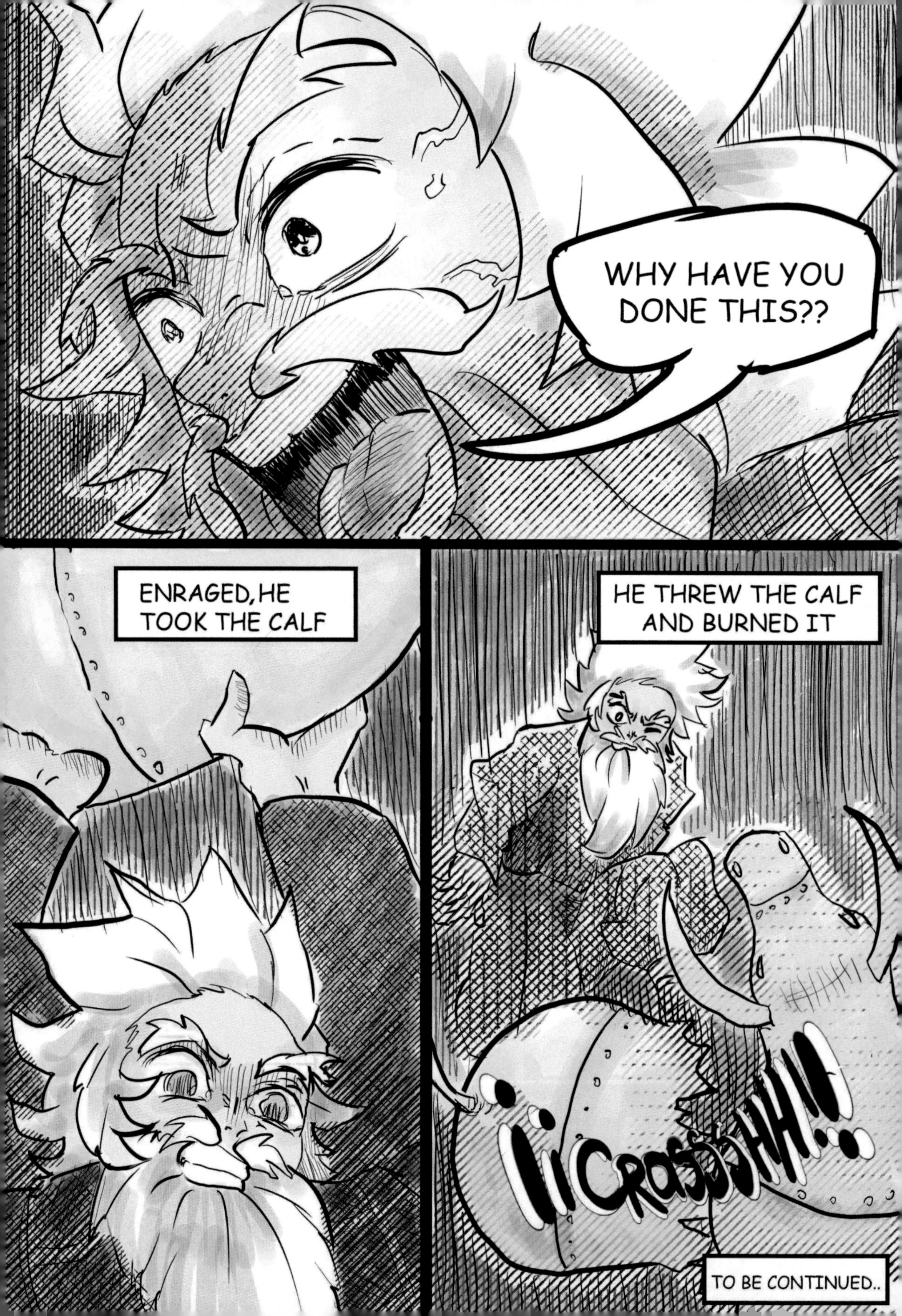
WHY HAVE YOU DONE THIS??
ENRAGED, HE TOOK THE CALF
HE THREW THE CALF AND BURNED IT
CRASSSHH!!
TO BE CONTINUED..

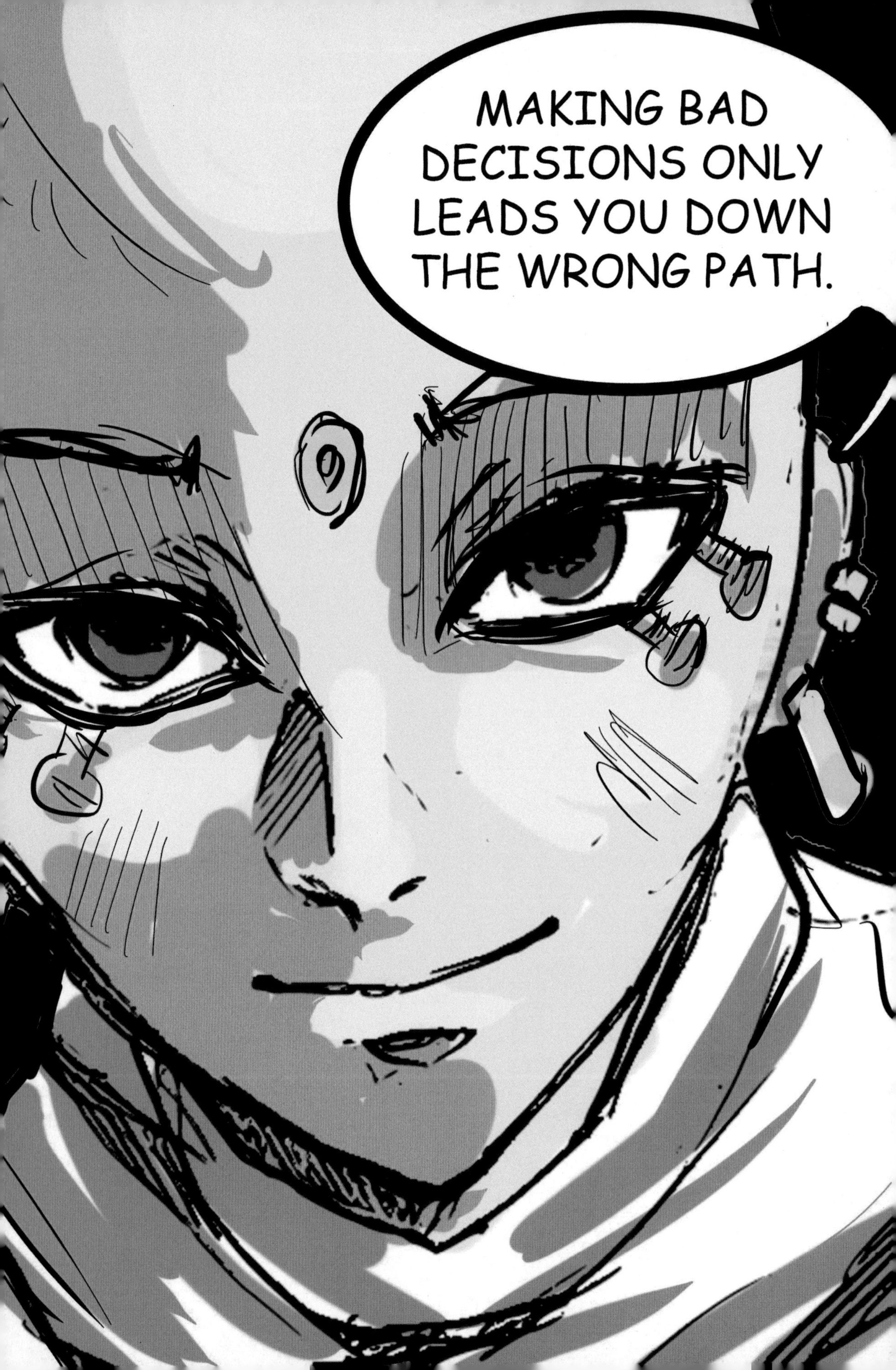
MAKING BAD DECISIONS ONLY LEADS YOU DOWN THE WRONG PATH.

DO NOT MISS ANY OF THE FUN, INCREDIBLE BIBLICAL ADVENTURES IN THE ANIME STYLE. EACH EPISODE WILL HELP YOU GROW IN THE KNOWLEDGE OF THE WORD OF GOD.

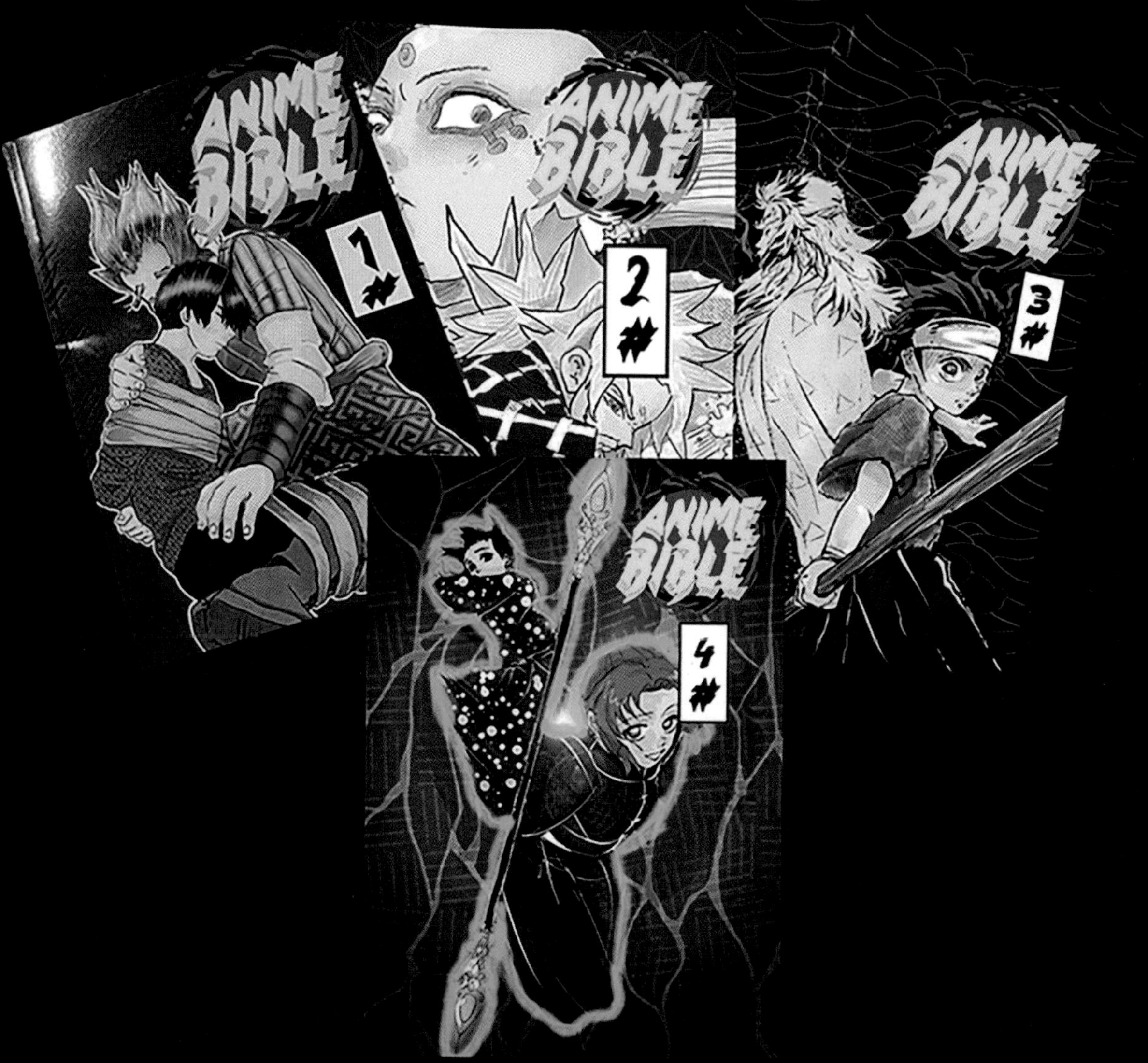
ANIME BIBLE
1 #
ANIME BIBLE
2 #
ANIME BIBLE
3 #
ANIME BIBLE
4 #

JAVIER ORTIZ/ FOUNDER AND CEO OF SUPERNESIS COMICS

JAVIER H. ORTIZ IS A COLOMBIAN WRITER WHO LIVES IN NEW YORK. HE HAS COVERED INSPIRATIONAL BOOKS, YOUNG READERS' BOOKS AND HE IS THE OWNER AND CREATOR OF SUPERNESIS COMICS. HE CURRENTLY TRAVELS AROUND THE WORLD DELIVERING CONFERENCES TO HELP PEOPLE DEVELOP THEIR HIGHEST POTENTIAL IN LIFE BASED UPON EXCELLENT PRINCIPALS. HE ALSO WROTE A BOOK THAT IS VERY WELL KNOWN BY THE NAME "THE WALKING WORD." HE ALWAYS LOOKS FORWARD TO ENRICHING PEOPLE WITH HIS NEW CREATIONS IN LITERATURE. HE IS THE AUTHOR OF "THE DIARY OF JOM JUNIOR", A BOOK FOR YOUNG READERS. MANY YOUNG READERS THROUGHOUT THIS BOOK BECOME AGENTS OF CHANGE WITH THE PURPOSE OF HELPING OTHERS TO MAKE A BETTER SOCIETY, AND A BRIGHTER WORLD.

ANTONIO SORIANO S ILLUSTRATOR/DESIGNER OF "MANGA BIBLE"

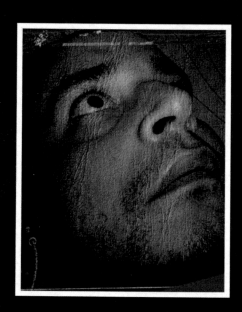

TRADITIONAL AND DIGITAL SCULPTOR, ILLUSTRATOR, GRAPHIC DESIGNER FROM BOGOTÁ COLOMBIA, AND LOVER OF LIFE AND ITS CREATURES, ESPECIALLY DOGS AND CATS, FROM AN EARLY AGE HE FELL IN LOVE WITH PENCILS AND MOLDABLE MATERIALS, COLORED PENCILS AND PLAY-DOH FORGED HIS PASSION FOR PLASTIC ARTS AND WITH MORE THAN 20 YEARS OF EXPERIENCE, TODAY HE OFFERS HIS CLIENTS QUALITY WORK AND, ABOVE ALL, MADE WITH THE LOVE AND DEDICATION OF A LIFETIME.

HE CURRENTLY WORKS AS A SCULPTOR DESIGNING TOYS AND COLLECTIBLES FOR PRIVATE COLLECTORS AND EMERGING COMPANIES SUCH AS SUPERNESIS COMICS, WITHOUT NEGLECTING PENCILS. HE IS AN ART CONSULTANT FOR COMPANIES, AND HE IS DEDICATED TO GRAPHIC ARTS AND COLLECTING COLLECTIBLES SUCH AS YAMATO TOYS.

SUPERNESIS

FOLLOW US ON INSTAGRAM!

INSTAGRAM.COM/SUPERNESIS
ADD №SUPERNESIS TO YOUR POST!

FOLLOW US ON FACEBOOK!

FACEBOOK.COM/SUPERNESIS

Made in the USA
Columbia, SC
27 June 2023

19535553R00020